Presented to my grandchild,

_____

Grandmother's Wonderful Wisdom

WRITTEN BY
Karen Hill

ILLUSTRATED BY
Maren Scott

J COUNTRYMAN®

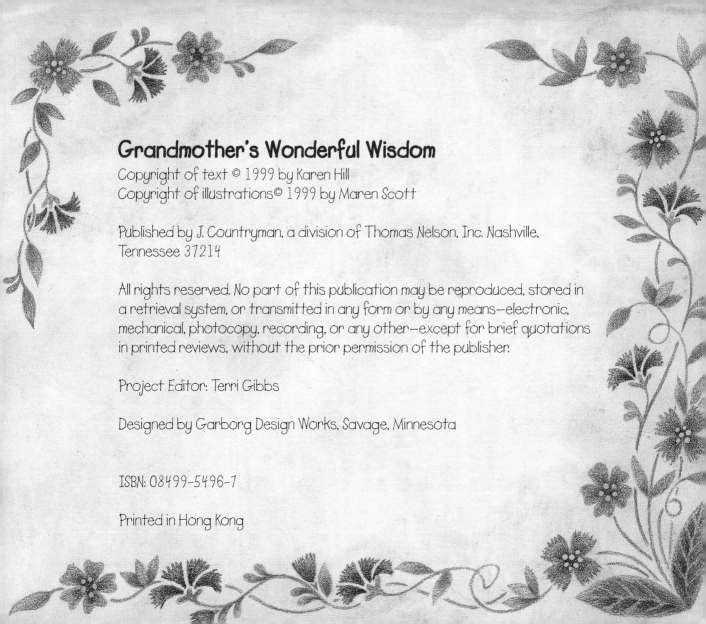

Grandmother's Wonderful Wisdom

Published by J. Countryman, a division of Thomas Nelson, Inc. Nashville, Tennessee 37214

Project Editor: Terri Gibbs

Designed by Garborg Design Works, Savage, Minnesota

ISBN: 08499-5496-7

Printed in Hong Kong

To Lois Jeane Cayce Davis

and Vernene Campbell Hill–

for grandmothering my children

with remarkable wisdom

and unending love.

–Karen Hill

Dear Grandmother,

Someone once wrote:

> I saw tomorrow look at me
> from little children's eyes;
> and thought how carefully we'd teach
> if we were really wise.

Wouldn't you love to pour everything you've learned from life into your grandchild? Wouldn't you delight in sharing the wisdom that comes from living and experiencing, from failing and succeeding, from learning how to make friends and how to be a friend?

My hope is that this book will help you do just that. As you read through the practical proverbs for living, consider how you can further explain their truths by examples from your own life.

By recording some of your life experiences and writing a few tidbits of your own wisdom in this journal, you'll provide a one-of-a-kind book for your grandchild—a gift that will become a treasured family heirloom.

May you and your grandchild be blessed as you retrace your life's path.

Blessings,

Karen Hill

Dear Grandchild,

Welcome to Grandmother's Wonderful Wisdom!

This book is a collection of wise sayings. And it contains many thoughts and ideas to help you on your life's journey. But it's not like any other book—it's been written just for YOU!

I hope it's as special to you as you are to me! I've added lots of my own stories and thoughts, remembrances, and words of blessing for you.

So, consider this book your personal treasure box of wisdom. I hope you'll discover some insights that will help you—and lots of love and laughter while you're at it.

My heart goes with you on your journey!

Lovingly,

Your Grandmother

So Many Grandmas!

Million of grannies, all in a row
Which one is mine? How will I know?

Ma-maw, Mi-ma, Nona, Oma,
Grandy, Grammers, Grandma, Gran

Tall ones, skinny ones, chubby ones, too,
All colors and sizes, old ones and new.

There's Mimi, Mahna, Gram, Granny,
Gramma, Namma, Mamma Sal, and Nanny.

A buffet of grandmas, each one a delight.
But how will I know? Which one is right?

Oh! There she is—see, over there?
I'd know her for sure, anytime, anywhere!

How did I know? It's easy you see—
She's the one with all the pictures of ME!!

—Karen Hill

9

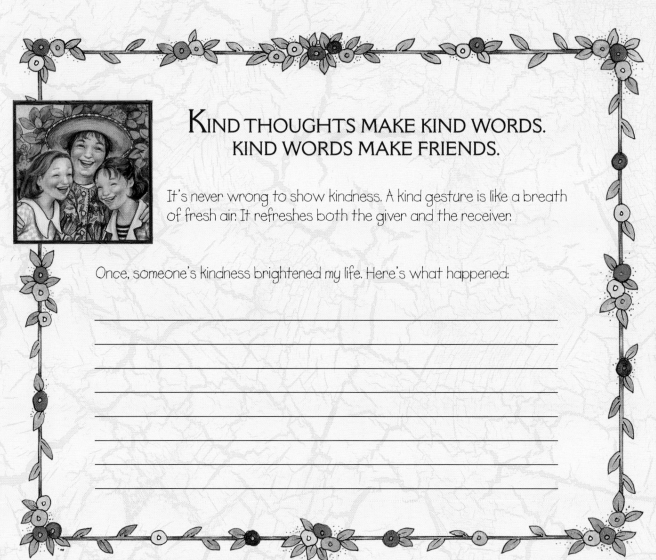

KIND THOUGHTS MAKE KIND WORDS. KIND WORDS MAKE FRIENDS.

It's never wrong to show kindness. A kind gesture is like a breath of fresh air. It refreshes both the giver and the receiver.

Once, someone's kindness brightened my life. Here's what happened:

_____

_____

_____

_____

_____

_____

_____

The words of a good person give life,
like a fountain of water.

PROVERBS 10:11

IF GOD HAD WANTED YOU TO BE JUST LIKE SO-AND-SO, HE WOULDN'T HAVE MADE YOU, YOU!

Don't try to be someone else! I'm glad you're YOU.

Would you like to know some of the reasons I think you're special?
Okay, here goes:

1. _____
2. _____
3. _____
4. _____
5. _____

6. _____
7. _____
8. _____
9. _____
10. _____

God has put something noble and
good into every heart His hand created.

—MARK TWAIN

If I could make the

perfect grandmother,

she would be just like mine.

She's perfect already.

(Actually, I have two of them.)

—MADISON GOMBERT, AGE 4

13

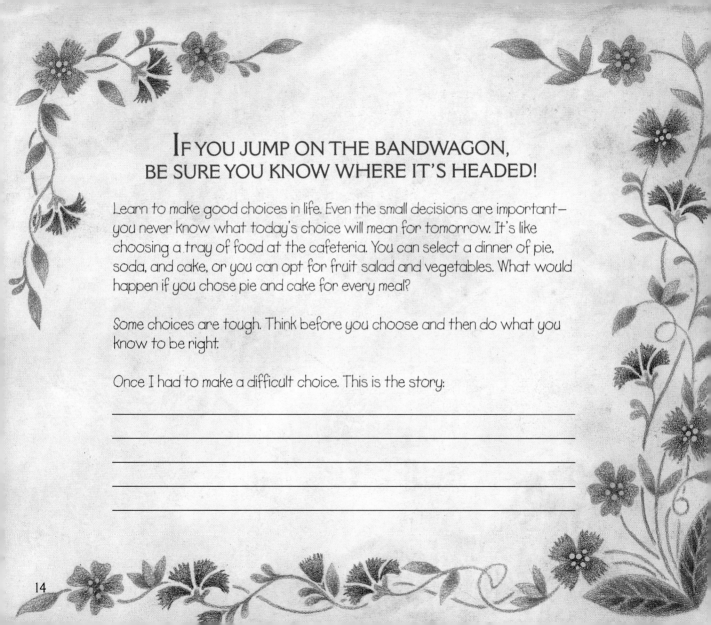

IF YOU JUMP ON THE BANDWAGON, BE SURE YOU KNOW WHERE IT'S HEADED!

Learn to make good choices in life. Even the small decisions are important— you never know what today's choice will mean for tomorrow. It's like choosing a tray of food at the cafeteria. You can select a dinner of pie, soda, and cake, or you can opt for fruit salad and vegetables. What would happen if you chose pie and cake for every meal?

Some choices are tough. Think before you choose and then do what you know to be right.

Once I had to make a difficult choice. This is the story:

_____

_____

_____

_____

_____

_____

_____

_____

_____

_____

_____

_____

_____

_____

_____

Destiny is not a matter of chance, it is a
matter of choice; it is not a thing to be
waited for, it is a thing to be achieved.

— WILLIAM JENNINGS BRYAN

15

grandmother

(American English)

16

GOD CREATED LAUGHTER! WHEN YOU GIGGLE OR SMILE, HEAVEN DANCES WITH JOY!

The Bible tells us "The joy of the LORD is your strength" (Neh. 8:10), and I know this is true. Smiles, laughter, and fun times with people we love make life grand!

I want to tell you about a funny, happy time in my life:

_____

_____

_____

_____

_____

_____

_____

I like to surprise my grandchildren with small gifts
we call "happies"–for absolutely no reason at all!

—LOIS JEANE DAVIS

17

GOD DOESN'T HOLD GRUDGES. HE DOESN'T WANT US TO, EITHER.

Forgiving someone who has hurt you is a tall order. But holding onto the hurt will only give you a grouchy heart. So work hard at forgetting the hurt and forgiving the person—you'll be much happier and so will your heart!

I know how tough it can be to forgive. This is how it happened to me:

_____

_____

_____

_____

_____

_____

_____

_____

_____

_____

_____

_____

_____

_____

_____

_____

_____

_____

_____

God pardons like a mother, who kisses the offense into everlasting forgiveness.

—HARRIET WARD BEECHER

STORMS DON'T LAST FOREVER.
RAINBOWS SHOW UP ONLY AFTER THE RAIN.
AND THE SUN SHINES BRIGHTEST AFTER
THE DARKEST NIGHT.

Life isn't always smooth sailing. There are tough times in everyone's life. But you may be surprised how much stronger you feel after the stormy season is over.

Here are some things you can do to help you get through a tough time:

1. _____
2. _____
3. _____
4. _____
5. _____

There are four things you can do
with the hurts that come into your life:
nurse them, curse them, rehearse them, or reverse them.

— PATRICK SHAUGHNESSY

"Grandmother"—love in any language.

mummi
(Finnish)

bobe
(Yiddish)

tutu
(Hawaiian)

zu-mu
(Chinese)

abuela
(Spanish)

ba
(Vietnamese)

yiayia
(Greek)

vovó
(Portugese)

21

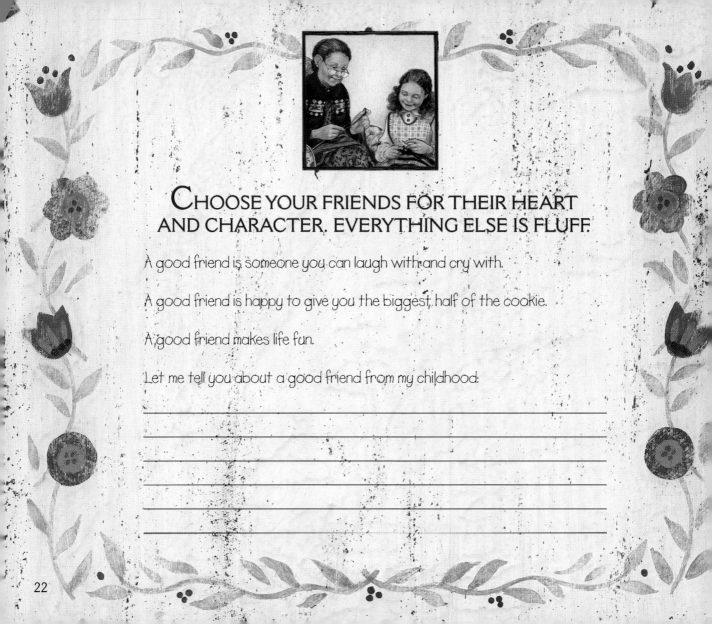

CHOOSE YOUR FRIENDS FOR THEIR HEART AND CHARACTER. EVERYTHING ELSE IS FLUFF.

A good friend is someone you can laugh with and cry with.

A good friend is happy to give you the biggest half of the cookie.

A good friend makes life fun.

Let me tell you about a good friend from my childhood:

_____

_____

_____

_____

_____

_____

_____

_____

_____

_____

_____

_____

_____

_____

_____

_____

Friendship is one of the sweetest joys of life.

— CHARLES HADDON SPURGEON

READ.
READ.
READ.

Treasure books. They will be your steady friends throughout life. They can transport you far away to visit many worlds and types of people.

Books are like brain fertilizer—they help your imagination to grow.

Here are some of my favorite books:

1. _____
2. _____
3. _____
4. _____
5. _____
6. _____

Reading is to the mind what exercise is to the body.

—RICHARD STEELE

Here are some books I think you might like to read:

1. _____

2. _____

3. _____

4. _____

5. _____

Reading takes you places you'll
probably never go in your life.

—AMIRA AMIN

DON'T LET COMPLIMENTS GO TO YOUR HEAD.

Humility goes against our human nature. We all want to believe the wonderful things people say about us. But remember this: God didn't create you to be glorified, but rather to glorify him!

Let me tell you about someone who has been an example of humility to me:

_____

_____

_____

_____

_____

_____

_____

_____

_____

_____

_____

_____

_____

_____

_____

_____

_____

_____

Pride will destroy a person;
a proud attitude leads to ruin.

—PROVERBS 16:18 NCV

grandmere
(French)

YOUR BODY IS THE EVIDENCE OF GOD'S CREATIVE GENIUS. TREAT IT WELL!

Take good care of your body! It has to last a lifetime! Brush and floss your teeth everyday. Exercise. Eat plenty of veggies.

Here are some other tidbits of advice for a healthy body:

_____

_____

_____

_____

_____

_____

_____

_____

We are God's workmanship.

EPHESIANS 2:10 NIV

Pray when you lose. Pray when you win.

You can pray to say "thanks." And you can pray to ask for help and comfort—God wants to hear from you, no matter what is happening in your life.

Let me tell you about a time when I said "thanks" to God and a time when I said "help!":

When I said "thanks":

_____

_____

_____

_____

_____

_____

_____

Prayer is the key of the morning
and the bolt of the evening.

— MATTHEW HENRY

When I said "help!":

_____

_____

_____

_____

_____

_____

_____

_____

_____

_____

ALWAYS TELL THE TRUTH.
EVEN WHEN IT HURTS.

Truthfulness is a strong indicator of good character, so practice truth-telling every day. If you learn to be truthful about small things, you will find it easy to be truthful about large things.

I remember a time when it was hard for me to tell the truth. Here's what happened…

_____

_____

_____

_____

_____

_____

Truthful lips endure forever.

—PROVERBS 12:19 NIV

YOUR SMILE IS THE FRONT PORCH OF YOUR HEART! LET IT BE WARM, WELCOMING, AND BRIGHT.

Isn't it fun to be around people who smile? Don't they make <u>you</u> want to smile? A smile makes you feel good inside.

Even when you don't feel like smiling, you can think of happy things and that will make you smile.

Here are some things that *make me smile every time I think of them*:

1. _____

2. _____

3. _____

4. _____

5. _____

6. _____

7. _____

8. _____

A smile costs nothing but gives much.

—ANONYMOUS

Speak to Older Folks—
It Makes Them Feel Young Again!

Don't ever pass up a chance to show a bit of kindness to anyone, but especially older people. A smile, a kind word, a gesture of consideration, an invitation to tell about their lives—there are many ways you can be a bright light in their day.

Don't be surprised if you find yourself blessed and encouraged by spending a moment in the presence of antiquity! Here are some ways you can encourage older folks:

1. _____
2. _____
3. _____
4. _____
5. _____

6. _____

7. _____

8. _____

9. _____

10. _____

You can multiply happiness by dividing it.

—ANONYMOUS

It is remarkable how, overnight,
a fat, elderly lady can learn to sit
cross-legged on the floor and play
a tin drum, quack like a duck,
sing all the verses of "The Twelve Days
of Christmas," make paper flowers,
draw pigs and sew on the ears of
severely injured teddy bears.

—HELEN EXLEY

DON'T GOSSIP . . . EVER . . . PERIOD.

Talking about other people's problems only leads to trouble.

When someone brings gossip to you, here are some ways to handle it:

1. _____
2. _____
3. _____
4. _____
5. _____
6. _____
7. _____

A gadabout gossip can't be trusted with a secret,
but someone of integrity won't violate a confidence.

PROVERBS 11:9 THE MESSAGE

TREAT YOUR FAMILY AS IF THEY WERE YOUR BEST FRIENDS. THEY ARE!

No one will ever care about you as much as your family does. Remember this during times of struggle and change. Be patient with your family. Always think the best of them. Be understanding and kind.

Spend time with your family and think of ways to show how you love them. God chose this family especially for you; hold them close and be grateful!

Here is a fond memory I have of each person in my family:

the person   the memory

_____   _____

_____   _____

_____   _____

_____   _____

the person

the memory

_____
_____
_____
_____
_____
_____
_____
_____

_____
_____
_____
_____
_____
_____
_____
_____

A family is a place where principles are
hammered and honed on the anvil of everyday life.

—CHARLES SWINDOLL

nyanya
(Swahili)

42

IT'S BETTER TO ERR ON THE SIDE OF GENEROSITY THAN TO BE GUILTY OF SELFISHNESS.

You don't have to be rich to be generous. Remember, everything you have comes from God. It really belongs to him, and he wants you to share your blessings with those who are less fortunate.

Giving to others not only makes them feel good, it makes us feel good too!

Here are some ways to share with others:

_____

_____

_____

_____

_____

_____

Share with God's people who need help.

—ROMANS 12:8

MONEY AND "THINGS" ARE POOR SUBSTITUTES FOR FAMILY, FRIENDSHIP, AND LOVE. DON'T PURSUE ONE AT THE EXPENSE OF THE OTHER.

True wealth isn't found in money and possessions. It is found in family, friends, faith in God, and a purposeful life.

Many people live their entire lives and never learn how to be truly rich. Let your life be wealthy in what matters—make each day valuable by what you put into it, not by how much money you make or how many trophies or belongings you collect.

In the treasure box of my life, this is my "gold":

1. _____

2. _____

3. _____

4. _____

5. _____

6. _____
7. _____
8. _____
9. _____
10. _____

A life devoted to "things" is a dead life, a stump;
a God-shaped life is a flourishing tree.

—PROVERBS 11:28, THE MESSAGE

DON'T LET A BUMP IN THE ROAD DERAIL YOUR DREAMS.

Just hold on tight to the end of the ride . . . and let your determination lead to confidence!

I remember one of the "bumps" in my life. Here's what I did and how it turned out:

_____

_____

_____

_____

_____

_____

_____

_____

ouma

(Afrikaans)

Challenges can be stepping stones or stumbling
blocks. It's just a matter of how you view them.

—ANONYMOUS

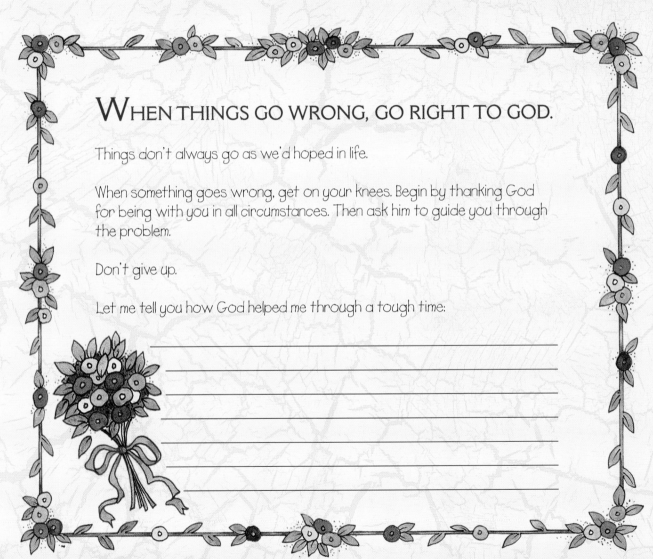

WHEN THINGS GO WRONG, GO RIGHT TO GOD.

Things don't always go as we'd hoped in life.

When something goes wrong, get on your knees. Begin by thanking God for being with you in all circumstances. Then ask him to guide you through the problem.

Don't give up.

Let me tell you how God helped me through a tough time:

_____

_____

_____

_____

_____

_____

Here is a list of some verses from the Bible that will encourage you in the hard times.

1. _____
2. _____
3. _____
4. _____
5. _____
6. _____
7. _____
8. _____

The human spirit is never finished when it is defeated...
it is finished when it surrenders.

—BEN STEIN

mam-gu

(Welsh)

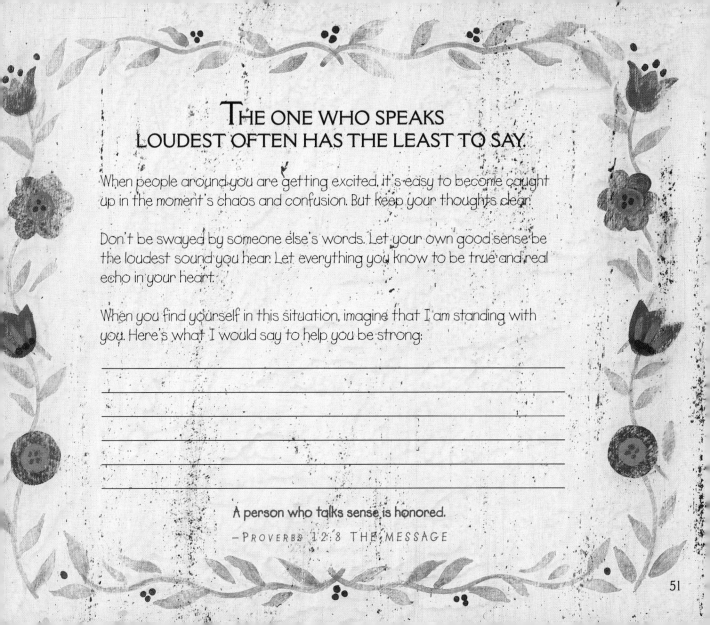

THE ONE WHO SPEAKS LOUDEST OFTEN HAS THE LEAST TO SAY.

When people around you are getting excited, it's easy to become caught up in the moment's chaos and confusion. But keep your thoughts clear.

Don't be swayed by someone else's words. Let your own good sense be the loudest sound you hear. Let everything you know to be true and real echo in your heart.

When you find yourself in this situation, imagine that I am standing with you. Here's what I would say to help you be strong:

_____

_____

_____

_____

_____

A person who talks sense is honored.

—PROVERBS 12:8 THE MESSAGE

HAVING TO MAKE DECISIONS MEANS YOU'RE GROWING UP . . . BUT THINK CAREFULLY BEFORE YOU MAKE THEM.

Decisions are good tools for learning. Even bad decisions help us learn. But before you make a decision, consult your heavenly Father.

A good decision I made was . . .

_____

_____

_____

_____

_____

_____

_____

_____

_____

A bad decision I made was . . .

_____

_____

_____

_____

_____

_____

_____

_____

Trust in the Lord with all your heart and lean not on your own understanding;
in all your ways acknowledge him, and he will make your paths straight.

PROVERBS 3:5–6 NIV

SHARE EAGERLY WITH OTHERS.
IT WILL MAKE YOUR HEART DANCE.

Want to energize your heart? Share.

Want to serve others? Share.

Want to serve God? Share . . . with joy.

Here are some ways you can share with others:

1. _____

2. _____

3. _____

You have not lived today
until you have done
something for someone
who can never repay you.

—PAUL BUNYAN

4. _____
5. _____
6. _____
7. _____
8. _____
9. _____
10. _____

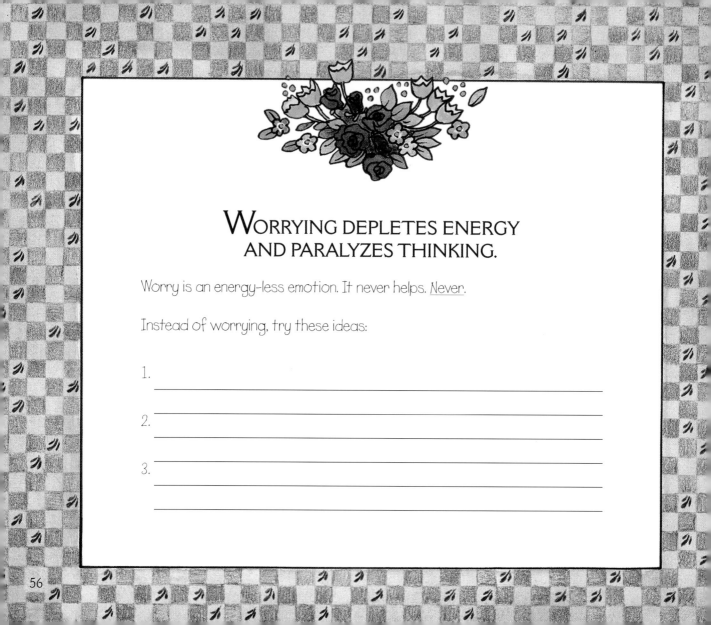

Worrying depletes energy and paralyzes thinking.

Worry is an energy-less emotion. It never helps. <u>Never</u>.

Instead of worrying, try these ideas:

1. _____
_____

2. _____
_____

3. _____
_____
_____

bunica (Romanian)

4. _____

_____

5. _____

_____

6. _____

_____

Worry does not help anything, but it hurts everything.

—GENERAL GEORGE S. PATTON

babushka
(Russian)

Grandmothers are people
who start out like us and
then they get old.

—ELIZABETH ANTHONY, AGE 4

58

ALWAYS REMEMBER THE WALKS YOU TOOK WHEN YOU WERE LITTLE.

Here's what I remember about one walk when I was a little girl . . .

_____

_____

_____

_____

_____

_____

_____

_____

Joy is the serious business of heaven.

−C. S. LEWIS

We have two rules when
the grandchildren come:
We only do it if it's fun and
we only eat it if we like it!

—CHARLENE CARPENTER

GROW A GRATEFUL HEART. IT'S THE BEST WAY TO ALWAYS SEE THE WORLD SUNNY-SIDE-UP.

Always be thankful: to God, to your family, to all those whose paths cross yours in life.

Here are a few of the many things I'm grateful for:

_____

_____

_____

_____

_____

_____

Not what we say about our blessings but how we
use them is the true measure of our thanksgiving.

— W. T. PURKISER

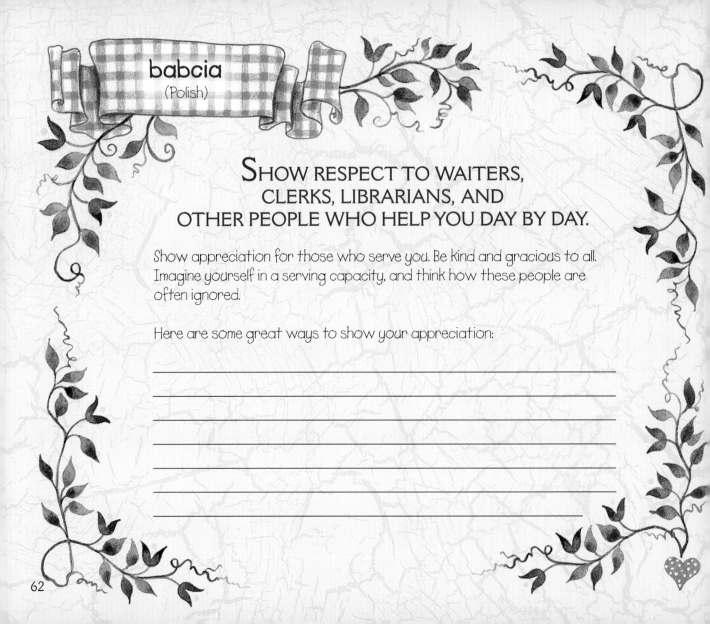

babcia
(Polish)

SHOW RESPECT TO WAITERS, CLERKS, LIBRARIANS, AND OTHER PEOPLE WHO HELP YOU DAY BY DAY.

Show appreciation for those who serve you. Be kind and gracious to all. Imagine yourself in a serving capacity, and think how these people are often ignored.

Here are some great ways to show your appreciation:

_____

_____

_____

_____

_____

_____

Always be a little kinder
than necessary.

—James M. Barrie

TRUST GOD'S HEART AS MUCH AS HE LOVES YOURS.

Never, ever doubt your heavenly Father's love. It's the one constant in your life, no matter what else happens.

Here is my prayer for your life:

_____

_____

_____

_____

_____

_____

_____

_____

Faith sees the invisible, believes the incredible, and receives the impossible.

—DAG HAMMARSKJOLD

Here is a special verse of Scripture or thought for your life:

grossmutter
(German)

WHATEVER YOU MAY LOSE IN LIFE,
NEVER LOSE HOPE.
IT COSTS NOTHING, BUT ITS VALUE IS PRICELESS.

Hope is an easy thing to lose, and once lost, even harder to regain.
Determine to be hopeful in all situations.

One time I nearly lost hope. Here's my story:

_____

_____

_____

_____

_____

_____

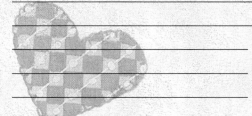

_____

_____   Hope is the thing with feathers
                                 That perches in the soul,
_____   And sings the tune without the words,
                                    And never stops at all.

                                 —EMILY DICKINSON

BEING A GOOD LISTENER MEANS LISTENING WITH YOUR HEART.

I think the best way to learn how to be a good listener is to spend time with someone who is a good listener.

When I want someone to listen closely to me, this is the person I go to, and here's why . . .

_____

_____

_____

_____

_____

_____

_____

There is a grace of kind listening, as well
as a grace of kind speaking.

—FREDERICK WILLIAM FABER

GET RID OF CONFLICTS!
RESOLVE THEM AS QUICKLY AS POSSIBLE.

But do it carefully and thoughtfully. Before you speak up, think through the problem. Before you assume the other person is at fault, stop and consider whether there is something you need to apologize for.

Let me tell you how I once resolved a conflict in my life:

_____

_____

_____

_____

_____

_____

_____

Handle words carefully, for they have
more power than atomic bombs.

—PEARL HURD

LOOK WITH EYES OF JOY AND WONDER WHEN YOU SEE FUZZY PUPPIES, FRESH FLOWERS, AND EVEN BUMPY GREEN FROGS.

God has made a beautiful world for us to enjoy.

Look around you. It's pretty amazing isn't it?

If I could plan a perfect day enjoying nature, this is what I'd like to do:

_____

_____

_____

_____

_____

_____

_____

Nature is the art of God.

— SIR THOMAS BROWNE

If only the Ugly Duckling had had a grandmother, he
need never have suffered. She of course, would have
seen at once that he was swan material.

— PAM BROWN

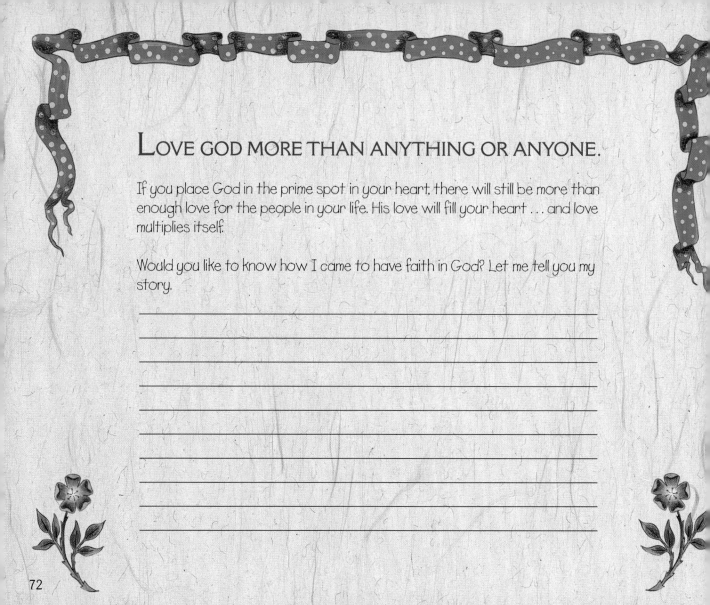

LOVE GOD MORE THAN ANYTHING OR ANYONE.

If you place God in the prime spot in your heart, there will still be more than enough love for the people in your life. His love will fill your heart . . . and love multiplies itself.

Would you like to know how I came to have faith in God? Let me tell you my story.

_____

_____

_____

_____

_____

_____

_____

_____

_____

_____

_____
_____
_____
_____
_____
_____
_____
_____
_____
_____
_____

grandmum

(Australian)

You only love God as much as the person you love the least.

—ANONYMOUS

shema'suna
(Navajo)

FILE AWAY FAILURES
IN THE DRAWER MARKED "YESTERDAY."

Mistakes help us grow and learn. But dwelling on them can be destructive, a waste of time.

So learn the lesson; then put the pain away.

This is a lesson I learned from a mistake:

_____

_____

_____

_____

_____

_____

_____

_____

In the middle of difficulty lies opportunity.

—ALBERT EINSTEIN

THE GREATEST POWER WITHIN YOU IS YOUR FAITH IN GOD.

Tap into that power source every day.

Set aside time each day to spend alone with God.

When you have a quiet time with God, here are some things you can do:

1._____

_____

2._____

_____

3._____

_____

4._____

_____

The LORD is close to everyone who prays to him, to all who truly pray to him.

PSALM 145:18 NCV

A DAY OF REST IS A GODLY THING (AND A GOOD THING) TO DO.

God rested, and so should we. Don't you agree?

Give your spirit and your body a chance to recharge once a week.

Can you think of some ways to find a time and place to rest?

Here's how I do it:

_____

_____

_____

_____

_____

_____

_____

_____

Rest is the sweet sauce of labor.

—PLUTARCH

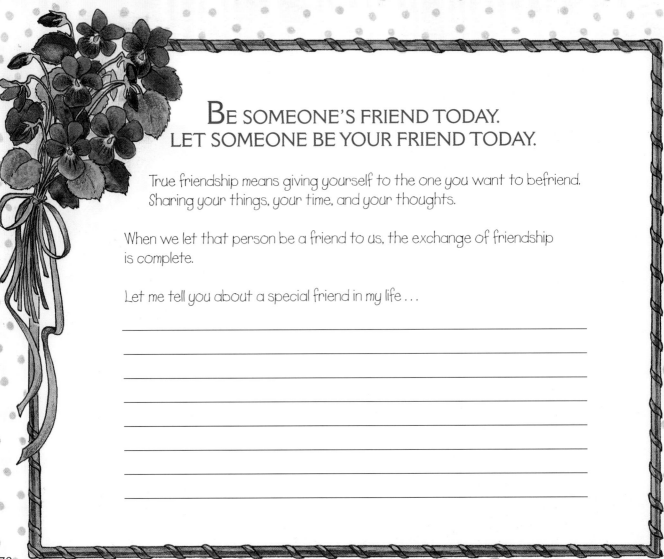

BE SOMEONE'S FRIEND TODAY.
LET SOMEONE BE YOUR FRIEND TODAY.

True friendship means giving yourself to the one you want to befriend. Sharing your things, your time, and your thoughts.

When we let that person be a friend to us, the exchange of friendship is complete.

Let me tell you about a special friend in my life . . .

_____

_____

_____

_____

_____

_____

_____

Let me tell you about some of the fun
things we've done together:

_____

_____

_____

_____

_____

_____

_____

_____

_____

We cannot hold a torch to light another's path without brightening our own.

— BEN SWEETLAND

DO GOOD DEEDS IN SECRET.

When you do something good, the reward is the good feeling you have inside yourself. No one else even needs to know about it.

If you plan to do a good deed simply for the praise and approval of other people, back up and start over. Plan to do it in secret!

Here are some good "secret" deeds you might like to try:

1. _____

_____

2. _____

_____

3. _____

_____

Real generosity is doing something nice for someone who'll never find it out.

—FRANK M. CLARK

4. _____

_____

5. _____

_____

6. _____

_____

7. _____

_____

oma
(Dutch)

LAUGH. A LOT.

Always laugh at other people's jokes. And be willing to laugh at yourself, especially when the joke is on you!

This is the funniest joke anyone ever pulled on me:

_____

_____

_____

_____

_____

_____

_____

Laughter is the shortest distance between two people.

—VICTOR BORGE

Don't demand more of others than you expect of yourself.

It's so easy to judge others. But be careful of the yardstick by which you measure others. You have to use this same yardstick to measure yourself.

When we are tempted to judge others, it helps to remind ourselves that we still need to grow and improve ourselves.

Here are some things I still need to improve in my life:

_____

_____

_____

_____

_____

_____

If you judge people, you have no time to love them.

—Mother Teresa

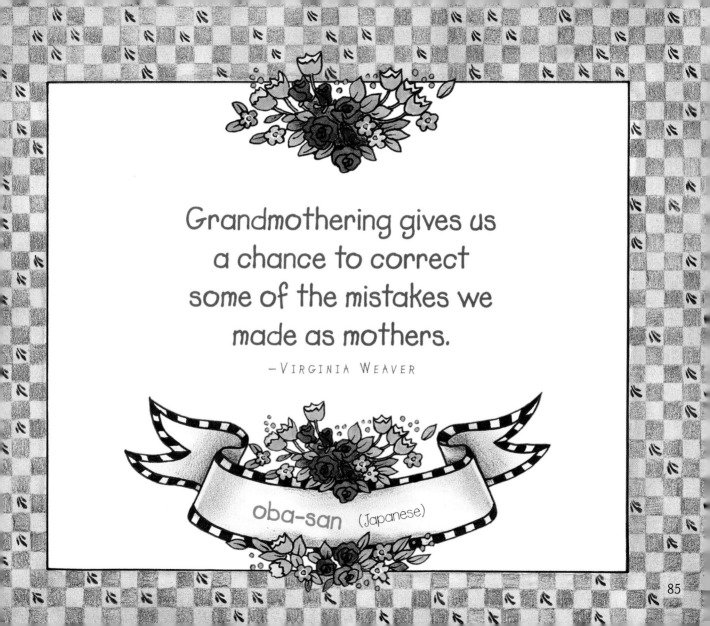

Grandmothering gives us
a chance to correct
some of the mistakes we
made as mothers.

—VIRGINIA WEAVER

oba-san (Japanese)

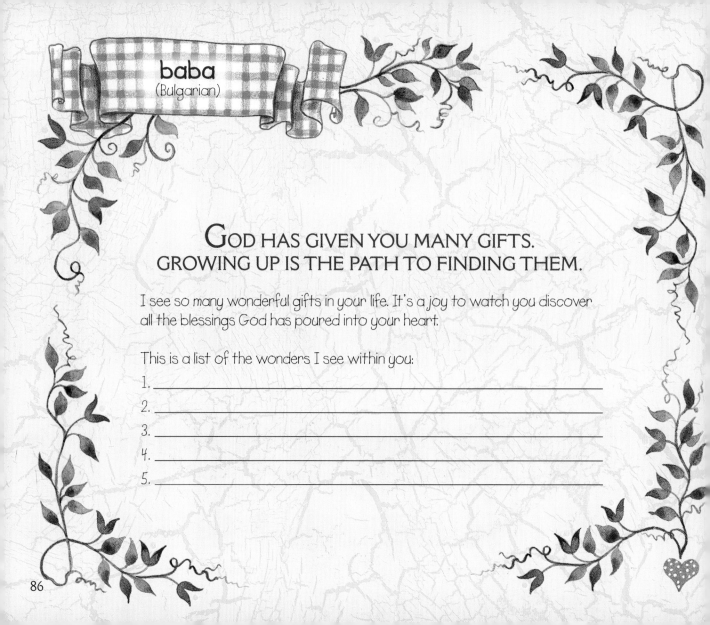

baba
(Bulgarian)

GOD HAS GIVEN YOU MANY GIFTS.
GROWING UP IS THE PATH TO FINDING THEM.

I see so many wonderful gifts in your life. It's a joy to watch you discover all the blessings God has poured into your heart.

This is a list of the wonders I see within you:

1. _____
2. _____
3. _____
4. _____
5. _____

6. _____

7. _____

8. _____

9. _____

10. _____

Thanks be to God for his indescribable gift!

2 CORINTHIANS 9:15

HONOR YOUR FAMILY TRADITIONS. THEY CONNECT YOU TO ALL THE GENERATIONS BEFORE YOU.

One thing that makes your family special from every other family is the traditions you keep—traditions that began long before you were born. Passing these traditions along to the next generation will connect you to your family in the past and your family in the future.

Here are some of our family traditions that I hope you'll continue with your own family someday:

_____

_____

_____

_____

_____

_____

_____

_____

_____

_____

_____

_____

_____

_____

_____

_____

_____

_____

Loving relationships are a family's best
protection against the challenges of the world.

— BERNIE WIEBE

inua
(Eskimo)

YOU CAN MAKE A DIFFERENCE IN THIS WORLD. NOW GO, AND DO IT! (I'M RIGHT BEHIND YOU!)

You are special to me, and you're special to God. Think about the gifts he has given you. How can you use those gifts to make this world a better place?

I'll pray for you and encourage you.

These are my hopes and dreams for you . . .

_____

_____

_____

_____

_____

_____

Commit to the Lord whatever you do, and your plans will succeed.

PROVERBS 16:3

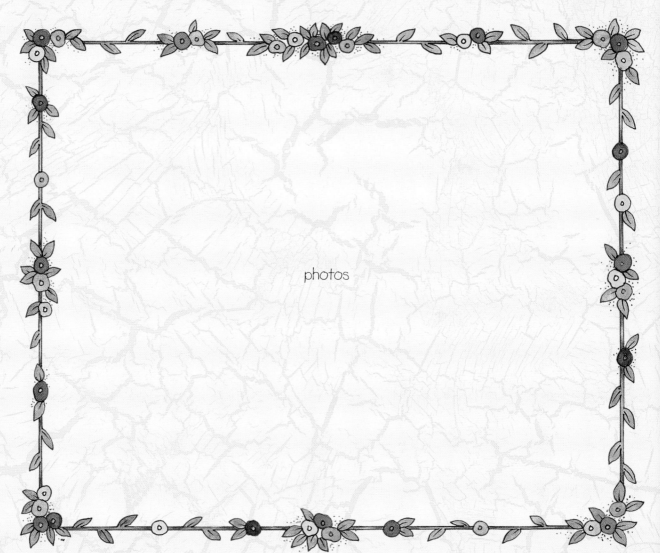

photos

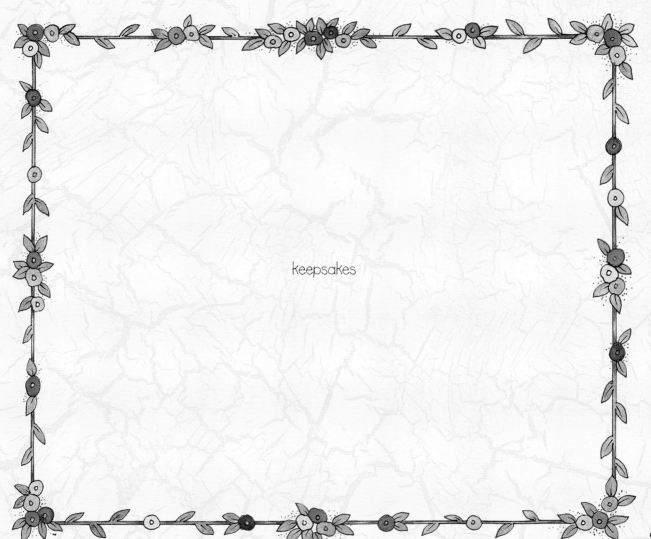

keepsakes

photos

keepsakes

Rosemary for remembrance

Grandparents are to be thanked for showing a child, at the beginning of life, the gentleness of the end of life.

—CHARLES AND ANN MORSE